What's Wrong With Her?

A Black Man's Guide To Understanding, Evaluating & Healing The Black Woman Vol 3

By: Aaron Fields

ISBN: **978-1-953962-35-5**

CONTENTS

<u>Something To Think About Before You Read</u>

It is not the black woman's job to change, it is our job as black men to change. Once we change ourselves and our environments, that's when they'll change------------Aaron Fields

Word From The Author

Gentlemen, it is apparent that there is a lot of chaos taking place in this society and within our culture. It is fair to say that a major reason there is so much entropy in the black community is because we are not unified and we're not on one accord. As black men, if we refuse to uplift ourselves and better our lives, we will continue to contribute to the problems that are taking place in our community.

As it pertains to black women, we know that many of them are going through a lot mentally, physically, emotionally, financially, and spiritually. It would be foolish for us as men to amplify their issues by purposely bringing more instability and negativity into their lives. In order to adjust to our environment and improve our culture, we must recalibrate our mindset. We cannot leave it up to the black women in our community to solve the problem. It is not their job to take on all the burden and the responsibilities.

For the most part, women have a survival mindset. If you place a woman in an environment that is foreign to her, there is a greater chance of her seeking out a man with power and stability. Keep in mind there is nothing wrong with a woman wanting to seek a man that has his life in order because that's part of her nature.

Although our women can sometimes be problematic, we must keep in mind that there are still a lot of descent black women out here. Most of it comes down to how we choose to value and conduct ourselves as black men. If the woman continues to be a problematic person in your life, all you need to do is move on from the relationship and stop waiting around complaining, begging and expecting her to change her behavior towards you. It's not the woman's job to change. In fact, it is our job as men to change. The more we start to better ourselves as black men, the more respect we'll start to get from our women and society. Always remember if we want to create a better community and develop a better culture, it has to start with us.

Let's Start With Leadership

When it comes to understanding the issues between black men and black women, it's always essential to address the importance of leadership. Part of the reason why you see most black women angry and resentful towards black men is because too many black men put themselves in situations where the women have to take care of them like a child. The black man must understand that if you want the woman to take care of you like a child, she's going to start treating you like a child.

Why does the black man feel less than? Why does the black man feel marginalized? It's because the black man doesn't value himself. Gentlemen, never allow yourself to feel marginalized. Never play a role in your emasculation and never deprive yourself of your manly duties.

Always remember that you cannot blame a woman for being a woman. Women by nature seek men who at the very least know how to take care of themselves and are capable of taking care of a family. The problem with a lot of you guys is that most of you depend too much on the women to speak life into you and uplift your spirit. Now don't get me wrong having a woman who is helpful and supportive is a blessing. However, women are looking for men who know how to pick themselves up on their own when they're down. Keep in mind, the woman is looking for you to be self-motivated, a self-starter and a leader.

As it pertains to leadership, many black women in their heart of hearts do not want to carry that burden of being a leader. In fact, most of them lead because their circumstances force them to. This creates a lack of trust in black men as a collective. In order to rebuild that trust, more black men have to demonstrate strong leadership abilities, be more discipline, as well as be goal oriented. Now does this mean all black men need to be millionaires? No not necessarily. However, I do believe it's important for black men to develop a healthy mind and a wealthy spirit. In other words, you must know what you want out of life. It's not the woman's job to figure that out for you. Believe it or not, the woman is going to be looking to you for inspiration. No matter how smart and successful these women are, most of them would love to receive inspiration, and wisdom from a man. It is natural for a woman to look for a man who is healthy and stable in every aspect of his life (mentally, emotionally, financially, physically, and spiritually).

Stop Letting Her Take Over

So many men (particularly black men) are so accustomed to having women preside over them. It's getting to the point where they want these women to be like their mothers. Black men must understand that it's not healthy to think this way because women will start to resent you and treat you with less respect. When the black man no longer believes in himself and he's relying on the woman to take him to the promise land, he's setting a poor example and creating a poor self-image for his children, especially his son.

Relying on women to do everything for you is a sign of weakness. Black men as a collective have to do a better job at putting their foot down when comes it to taking the lead and having an end game. If black men continue to allow black women to take charge in the community, this will trickle down into the household. Once this happens, you can't blame the black woman. If you allow her to take ownership of the community, you can't be surprised if she carries that same mentality into the household. That's why it's important for black men to stop being so weak minded. Although it's important to love and honor the black woman, it's not fruitful to view her as your lord and savior.

In life, you conduct yourself based on how you think. Unfortunately, a lot of black men think and act like women. Therefore, you start to see more black female leadership. While some of you may think this is a good thing, one can make the argument that the push and promotion of black female leadership is a manifestation of the black man's weakness. In other words, seeing more black female leadership in the community indicates that black men don't have a solution to the problems in the community and they can't get the job done. The black man is doing his community a disservice when he cries, complains, and throws a temper tantrum. Instead of black men wasting their time hoping and begging for change, it'll be best to create a plan of action.

Since many black men have been trained to act and think like women, they will have a difficult time developing a vision for their life and constructing a macrocosmic plan. If the black man can't be trusted in the household and in his community, he will not be trusted as a teacher, a coach, a manager, an executive or a CEO. The black man has to change how he views himself in order to change how other groups of people view him.

Demonstrate Discipline

In order to create change, one must use discretion and utilize great discipline. Discipline tends to be a major issue for a lot of black men, especially when it comes to dealing with women (including black women). Unfortunately, too many black men have an unhealthy infatuation with women and too many of them allow the matriarchal energy to consume them.

As a collective, black women don't look up to black men. Why is that the case? Well to answer that question, maybe it's because the black man is not giving the black woman anything to look up to. It's imperative for the black man to be a beacon of hope and a source of inspiration for the black woman. Now does that mean the black woman will always look up to you? No, it doesn't. Believe it or not, there are some women out here that don't look up to upstanding men.

Sadly, in the black community, the women don't look to men for leadership, only for sex and manipulation. Why is that? Well, it's largely because that's what we as black men allow. Sometimes to get respect from our women, we must tell them "No", especially when it comes to sex. Let's be honest, a lot of black men love to promote and advertise sex. Too many black men love talking about their sexual experiences with women. Now is sex a terrible thing? No, not necessarily. However, it becomes problematic if sex is the only thing you talk about and partake in. What else can the black man do? Does he have any goals? Is he making positive contributions in his community? Is the black man working on becoming the best version of himself? Can he properly love and guide the women and children in his community?

The reason I'm asking these questions is because the black man has so much to live for. It's important for the black man to not partake in certain things that can potentially stunt his growth and hinder his ability to achieve great things in this world. As I mentioned earlier, sexual discipline is one of the most important things black men should consider working on. Sometimes you're going to encounter certain women that want you to inseminate them. Why am I mentioning this? Well, if you are a man that's dealing with a woman that doesn't care if you're not using protection when it comes to sex, you as the man better care. If you're not ready or equipped to be a father to a child, it's important for you to take the necessary steps to make sure you're using protection. If you really want to make sure you're taking the appropriate steps to making sure she doesn't get pregnant, you can never go wrong with abstinence or abstaining yourself from sexual intercourse with her. Gentlemen, if you're not ready to have children, its okay to tell the woman "No". It doesn't matter how horny she is, and it doesn't matter if she attempts to shame you for it. If having children is something you don't want right now, it's okay to reject the woman. Now if you love the woman that you're with and she's sexually frustrated with you, ask her if she's open to partaking in other sexual activities with you other than sex. Keep in mind, there are so many ways to sexually satisfy a woman without having sex. As the man, use this opportunity to be more innovative and creative in your approach.

The Black Man Can't Be Afraid To Lead

A major reason most black men are afraid to lead is because most of them do not have worldly and spiritual intelligence. In fact, there are plenty of black men with worldly intelligence, but most of them don' t have the spiritual knowledge. In other words, most black men don't seek inspiration and guidance from the most high God.

Unfortunately, there are a number of black men in the community who are carnal minded. When you're carnal minded, your mind is not focused on spiritual things. As it pertains to interacting with women, being carnal minded can lead to a man developing an unhealthy infatuation with them. Part of the reason black men are in a low estate today is because they are not focused on the positive or spiritual aspects of life. In addition to that, many black men are not using the gifts and talents that God has given them.

One of the reasons a lot of black men are unwilling to lead is because they are scared to become discipline (struggles to overcome drug addictions, alcoholism, food, sex, anger issues, etc). Due to the lack of discipline from most black men, our community has embraced toxic ideologies and harmful ideas that have caused our culture to be more chaotic. Do not neglect the leadership responsibilities that you are supposed to take care of. Put down the weed, put down the alcohol, stop overindulging in sexual activities and focus more on optimizing your mind and elevating your spirit.

Please understand that a major reason most women do not respect black men is because a lot of black men are not doing their due diligence to becoming healthy and stable in every aspect of their life. Most women (black women) as a collective don't view black men as great leaders.

For women to respect you, you will need to demonstrate leadership capabilities and great decision-making skills in your everyday life. Not only it takes a long time to understand the women that you're dealing with, but it also takes a long time to understand yourself as a man, especially if you were raised in a chaotic environment.

Have High Expectations For Yourself

As I mentioned earlier in the first volume of this book, this is not about promoting a gender war agenda. A lot of guys are not going to like this, but I hold black men to a much higher standard than black women. Why? Well, because if we're going to call ourselves kings, we must exude strong leadership abilities and demonstrate kingship characteristics.

As it pertains to our women, it is in our best interest as men to not go back and forth with them all day. In other words, complaining about women and arguing with them is a complete waste of time and it's counterproductive. Once you have a better understanding of women, you'll most likely know what to do, how to conduct yourself and what not to tolerate when you're dealing with them.

When you start to develop a rapport with women, you must understand what you're getting yourself into. There are a lot of women out here with mental, psychological, and spiritual issues. Why is that the case? Because there are a lot of men with mental, psychological, and spiritual issues as well. Keep in mind it's not always the woman's fault. In fact, most of the issues taking place in society is our fault as men because we don't exhibit foresight, prudence, understanding, discernment and wisdom. As a man, if you don't feel confident in your abilities to demonstrate these characteristics in your day-to-day life, do not initiate a serious relationship with a woman. Although it's impossible to be perfect, it's always important to strive to become the best version of yourself everyday so that way the situations you run into with women won't be as severe.

As long you prioritize spiritual things and focus on becoming the best person you can be, you'll likely avoid most of the problems that women or other people will try to bring into your life. Once you become healthy and stable in every aspect of your life, you'll be able to enter most of your relationships already knowing what to expect from the woman and most importantly, yourself.

It's Okay To Get Rejected

In life, the man must be mentally prepared and accepting of the fact that he will one day face rejection, especially from a woman. Once the woman is no longer interested in you, it's time to leave the relationship. If the woman no longer wants to be with you, accept her wishes and walk away so you can move on with your life.

Since most young men are not receiving proper instructions on how to interact with women, they ultimately end up being ensnared. It's important for men to know that when you prioritize more important things in life, you'll successfully avoid many toxic situations with women. Once you enter in a relationship with a woman, you must understand what you're already going to expect from her. More importantly you must understand what to expect from yourself.

Sadly, there appears to be more stories in the mainstream media about men deciding to kill the woman, and/or themselves over a woman. When a man does this, it's a manifestation of his weakness and the lack of instructions and guidance he received. Too many men are becoming overly infatuated with women as opposed to focusing on maintaining a peaceful mind. Gentlemen, please understand that if the woman you're with is not concerned with your peace of mind as you are, it will be in your best interest to leave the relationship before things get worse.

In life we are going to get rejected sometimes and that's okay. If you like a certain woman and she doesn't like you back, that's okay. Sometimes a woman not liking you is a good thing. Why? It's because the universe (or God) is trying to save you from getting into a relationship and making a bad mistake. Keep in mind, some of these women out here do not have much to offer other than their physical appearance and it only makes you look weak as a man when you try to go back and forth with a woman that doesn't want to be with you.

Moving On After The Rejection

After taking and accepting the rejection, the goal for you as a man is to move on to a higher level of existence. Believe it or not, there are going to be better things out there waiting for you. Never get upset and angry with people that don't want you around. If they don't want you around, you shouldn't want to be around them. For example, if your job decides to get rid of you, that should motivate and galvanize you to elevate your life. As a man, you should be striving to be more discipline, self-motivated and self-contained.

What if the woman told you that she wants to move on from you? What if the woman tells you that the relationship is not working out and she wants to see other people? How are you going to respond? What will you do? If the woman wants to move on from you, please let her go and give her the opportunity to move on with her life.

As a man, it's imperative that you embrace solitude and view it as a necessity. Why? Well, because being by yourself is not only a beautiful thing, but eye-opening as well. Solitude also provides you the opportunity to be more reflective on the direction you want your life to go. Although no one is perfect, it is best to be healthy and stable in every aspect of your life before getting into a meaningful relationship with a woman. Even though it's important to love the woman, cherish her and honor her, you should never be overly infatuated with her. Keep in mind, some of these women will try to play games with your sanity if you allow them to. Not to be discouraging, but when dealing with women, always assume that it's a possibility the relationship might not work out. After a certain period, don't be surprised if the woman you're with starts to get bored of you. Is it possible that she is tired of your phone calls, and text messages? Perhaps she finds your daily routines to be predictable. Or maybe it's because you're not spicing things up in the relationship. Once the woman stops showing you the same love, respect, and courtesy that she was showing you initially, that is her way of telling you that you should start mentally preparing yourself to move on from the relationship.

The Best Way To Overcome A Breakup & Move On From A Rejection:

One of the best ways to overcome a major breakup or a rejection as a man is to develop a specific interest in something that is spiritually based. In other words, it is important for you guys to focus on something that will allow you to showcase your gifts and talents. Although women are wonderful and beautiful, your entire life cannot revolve around them. As a man you can't meet with a woman and automatically assume that your interaction with her is going to be a lifelong thing. Unfortunately, most guys think the relationship will last forever and then when it doesn't, the man loses his composer and ends hurting or killing the woman. Gentlemen, please focus on the things that matter in life. There is never a good reason to kill the woman and/or yourself over a relationship. If the woman breaks up with you, are you going to lose your mind, or are you going to move on to better things? Life is short, enjoy the moments you have left on this earth while you're still alive and well. Don't waste your time trying to be with women that don't want to be with you.

What are you gifted at? _____

_____

_____

_____

What do you want to do with your life?_____

_____

_____

_____

Where do you want to go? _____

_____

_____

_____

Take Your Time With Women

One of the best ways to protect yourself and the woman's sanity is for you as the man to take your time to develop yourself before getting into a committed relationship. If you're not interested in getting into a serious relationship with a woman, leave her alone. Are you still growing and maturing? Are you healthy and stable in every aspect of your life? If you're someone in the midst of figuring out who you are as a person, it might be in your best interest to not pursue a relationship with a woman at the moment.

The reason it's important to take your time in your relationships with women is because you never want to get ahead of yourself. Sadly, too many men get ahead of themselves and end up getting bitter and disappointed when the relationship doesn't work out. This explains why you see a lot of men blocking off opportunities for real love to enter their lives.

The last thing you want is to help create a child with a woman you don't love. It's important for a child to receive love from their parents. If you don't know how to love, the child is not going to know how to love, and the cycle will continue. That's why it's important to have a child with a woman when you're ready.

When interacting with women, you always want to make sure you search out every component of their character, so you have a better understanding of who you're dealing with. Keep in mind there are a lot of chaotic women out here that are seeking to create as much chaos as possible, especially if they feel scorned. You must take inventory of all the people that come into your life so that way when something bad happens, you won't be surprised.

Believe it or not, most people don't know how to love because they spend most of their time trying to see what they can take from the other person. When you're more concern on how you can help the other person that you're with, your interpersonal relationships will be more fulfilling and long-lasting. In addition to that, when you show that level of compassion and generosity towards the right person, you will always receive valuable things in return. Gentlemen, there are some women out here not worth dealing with. However, when you come across a descent woman that is exceptional and cares about you, please treat her well, do right by her, and don't take her for granted.

Call To Action

Making money off our dysfunction and hatred towards one another is not the way to go. It has gotten to the point where other groups of people are starting to speak on black issues as if they have a say so, even though it's clear that they have no skin in the game. One of the major keys to having a strong culture is to never allow outsiders to come in to dictate how the community functions. Always remember that an outsider with bad intentions will never have a personal investment in making you better. In fact, they are only invested in making you look worse than what you are.

It is clear that there is a lot of tension between black men and women. Although there are many discussions on how we communicate and treat one another, there are not that many discussions about creating a solution. To help bridge the gap between black men and black women, black men must play a significant role in the healing process. One can make the argument that there is a systemic and spiritual attack on us because the world knows that black people are much stronger when they're unified. Although that may be the case, we as black people need to stop blaming other people for the issues that transpire in our community. Yes, there is some level of societal engineering that is meant to ensure that we get the short end of the stick. However, once we understand the issues that are going on, we must take it upon ourselves to do something about it. We either learn how to adapt or perish.

It's imperative that black men and women develop a loving relationship with one another. In fact, our love for each other should ignite a spiritual spark in the community. However, in order for this to work, the black woman has to be willing to work with the black man and the black man must have the skills to build in some way shape or form. Even if you don't have the skills to do occasional domestic repairs, there are still certain things you can do to build. For example, if you are a good instructor, start teaching. If you're a good writer, start writing. Whatever it is that you can do to uplift your community and elevate your environment, go ahead and do it. One of the most important things you can do as a man is to have a vision for your life and start setting goals for yourself.

Stop Shaming Black Women For Their Accomplishments

Gentlemen, keep in mind that many black women are well accomplished and independent because they had to be. In other words, many of them didn't have a strong support system. A true successful man is not envy or jealous of a woman's success. Don't be intimated by her and her success and don't do anything to make her feel less than. Instead of going back and forth with women, continue to focus on your own goals and aspirations and figure out a way on how she can be a compliment to you.

Thoughts: _____

_____

_____

_____

_____

_____

_____

_____

_____

The Black Man Must Be The Savior

Gentlemen, when the woman knows that you're in your right state of mind, she's going to ask for your assistants when it comes to solving major issues because she views you as the leader. One of the signs of a positive relationship between a black man and a black woman is when the black man is properly guiding the black woman into a better life. Believe it or not, most women are seeking guidance from a man that has a vision for his life.

It's important to know that when it comes to our community, it is our job as black men to fix it and clean it up. In other words, it's not the white man's responsibility. We must stop seeking help from these other demographics and learn how to start solving the problems ourselves. Instead of getting mad at the white man and throwing a temper tantrum because he doesn't want to save you, start creating remedies and solutions to problems that will elevate the community and your people. The more you complain about a certain group of people, the more power you give them to have control over you. In life, you will not find fulfillment when you start seeking validation from other people.

In order for the black community to be successful, the black man must be willing to be the savior for himself and for his people. If you're a black man that has no interest in partaking in the salvation, this book is not for you. If all you care about is promoting harm, destruction, confusion, and violence, remove yourself from the community and go into isolation. We need more black men in our community that are filled with abundance, positivity and prosperity.

Be Honest With The Woman

As a man when it comes to being honest with other people, it's always important to be honest with yourself. When you're honest with yourself, you're more likely going to avoid negative situations. Believe it or not, being honest with yourself leads to you being honest with other people, especially to the ones you care about. Most people that are not honest with other people are usually not honest with themselves.

When you're interacting with women, make sure you have your ducks in a row and in order. In other words, you must understand the things that are important in your life. As a man, it's okay to prioritize your health and well-being over everything else. If you're in the midst of achieving something great in your life and you're focusing on becoming the best version of yourself, it's okay to tell women you're not seeking a serious relationship right now. For women to understand your situation, you must be honest with them, even if they don't like it.

Keep in mind that some women you interact with may not see you as a priority anyway. A major reason why a lot of you guys get heartbroken by women is because you put them on a pedestal. In other words, too many weak-minded men are overly infatuated with women. The moment the man gets his heart broken, he starts to lose his mind as well as his focus on the things that matter in his life. The reason most of you guys continue to have problems with women is because you're thinking and acting like women. It's important for the man to operate according to rules, high standards, and order. It's not healthy for a man to be impulsive and chaotic towards women.

If you know that you're not ready to be emotionally available for a woman but you still want to partake in sexual activities with her, please let her know as soon as possible so that way you can empower the woman by giving her the option to walk away from you if she doesn't want to participate. As a man, it's best that you don't lie or mislead the woman by letting her think that the two of you are in a relationship. Although women might get mad, you must also keep in mind that many of them appreciate and respect a man's honesty. Hell from a sexual standpoint, it might even turn them on. Gentlemen, when you're honest and you approach life in a straight and direct way, you'll avoid a lot of unnecessary situations. There is nothing wrong with embracing the truth.

Don't Become Obsessed With Her

There is a difference between loving your woman and becoming obsessed with her. As a man, never allow the woman to control you through emotional susceptibility. Unfortunately, a lot of women want a man to become obsessed with them until it finally happens. Many weak-minded men that become overly infatuated with women are usually the ones who take the relationship and the emotional dynamics too far to the point where it starts to turn into a domestic violence situation. Sadly, in some cases, it leads to the man killing the woman.

The man must understand that the woman is not his God. There is no shame in moving on from the woman. That's why it's important for you guys to have aspirations that are spiritually based or at the very least develop a goal that will put you in a promising position and will allow you to showcase your inner talents. Gentlemen, please understand that your entire life cannot revolve around women.

There are too many men out here with psychological and spiritual problems. That's why it's important for men to seek help when they need it. Stop developing anger and resentment towards women and learn how to move on from them. If the woman you're with is not treating you well, leave the relationship and find someone else who respects you. Lastly don't be afraid to be by yourself for a little bit. Take the time to develop standards and expectations for yourself when it comes to creating a better life. Before bringing a woman into your life, make sure you are well equipped to be in a relationship with a woman that cares about you so you can make her life better.

Does She Respect You?

Respect is an important theme in a man's life. It's essential for men (black men in particular) to understand what it means to be respected and how to respect, especially when dealing with women. Unfortunately, a lot of men don't understand what it means to be respected because they're use to being disrespected. As it pertains to black men, many of them have been dealing with this problem since they were little boys. Whether it's their sister, auntie, cousin, or their mother, many young black boys are raised in toxic environments where they become accustomed to being marginalized and talked down to in public.

As these young boys get older, they start to believe that getting disrespected is a normal part of the conversation when communicating with women. Sadly, too many men don't know or understand what a healthy dialogue is supposed to look like. Therefore, these boys and men suffer in silence. Please understand that tolerating disrespect is not healthy. So many black men are dead or in prison because a lot of them agreed to the rules of engagement that were established for them during their youth and by many of the black matriarchal figures they grew up with. In addition to that, many of these black boys grew up in fatherless homes or with weak minded black men that couldn't teach them about the importance of having healthy communication skills when interacting with a woman.

Gentlemen, if you're with a woman that you respect but she doesn't respect you, cut her off and leave the relationship immediately before the relationship gets worse. The reason why these relationships become toxic is because both people don't know how to communicate with each other. That's why it's important for men to love and value themselves. Once you're able to love and value yourself as a man, it'll be easier for you to establish the rules of engagement in your interactions with women. The reason why it's important for men to set the tone in the relationship is because a lot of women have no idea what they're doing when they're speaking. In other words, many women are accustomed to being unabashed with what they say and how they say it to the point where they don't recognize when they're being disrespectful. While it's important for the woman to not be disrespectful, make sure that you're not being disrespectful to her. If the two of you have an issue, it's best to handle the situation in private as opposed to disrespecting each other in public.

The Inspiration Within

The black man must be a positive force in his community. The black man must also get in the habit of thinking on an optimal level. Lastly, the black man must stop looking to these other demographics for any type of impetus or inspiration. In other words, the black man must understand that these other demographics are the not the answer to his salvation.

In order to get to where we need to be as a community, black men as a collective must strive to become healthy and stable in every aspect of their life. Right now, the black community is experiencing a lot of trust issues between the men and women. For starters, the black man is not viewed as a leader or an administrator. Sadly, society (especially women) does not trust the black man when it comes to executing the laws in his own community. In order for the black man to reclaim his throne, he must learn how to love and respect himself.

It's important for the black man to not view himself as a source of destruction and confusion. In a society that doesn't care about you, it may not be in your best interest to look for sympathy from other people. It also makes your situation worse when you try to play the victim role instead of taking care of your personal responsibilities. This explains why our women don't respect us.

The black man must understand that he doesn't need help from these other demographics. He doesn't need their validation and he doesn't need a hug from them. The black man must build on his skills, understand his role in society, and he must be focused on elevating his life. In order for the black man to be a leader, a teacher, a guide, and a ruler over his community, he must start practicing righteous acts. In other words, it's essential for black men to live in a functional way so they can be an ensample and an inspiration for black women and the children.

Spiritual Servitude

One of the many ways black men can be a source of love and healing is through spiritual servitude. In other words, submitting yourself to God. A lot of black men don't have a purpose in life because they are lost and confused. Right now, the black man is in so much spiritual pain, he doesn't think to ask God for help. The reason why you hear black women say there are no black male leaders is because a lot of black men don't believe in themselves. To black women's credit, most of them have the ability to sense when something is off. The black man must keep in mind that the black woman will not follow him if he does not have a plan or a vision that will elevate his life and the people around him. If the black man is not giving the black woman anything to follow, she will just rather be by herself.

One of the major things black men want to make sure they don't fall victim to, is the idea of self-worship. When it comes to seeking spiritual understanding, it's important to never allege that you have all the answers. One of the best ways to express yourself to God is through spiritual servitude. From an earthly standpoint, we are all servants to one another. Somewhere along the line, we've lost the understanding of how to be a spiritual servant. This explains why there is so much entropy in our community.

The reason we lost this sense of spiritual servitude is because we no longer understand ourselves, our culture and our God. Therefore, we are now spiritless and no longer powerful. Once black men get a better understanding about the importance of humility and servitude, most of the toxic ideologies we adhere to in our community will go away. Never engage in self-worship and never view yourself as your own God. When you conform to this type of mentality, you'll most likely become angry, confused, and depressed. That's why it's important to seek knowledge and inspiration from the most high God.

As it pertains to the black community, we must understand our role. It's not wise to look for self-exaltation. In order for the black community to move forward in a positive direction, we must reject, rebuke and dismiss anyone that's trying to hinder our progress. Right now, a lot of us are mentally and spiritually ill. In order to heal, we must always be willing to look at ourselves in the mirror and self-scrutinize. By doing this, we will be able to avoid many of the pitfalls and stumbling blocks that will transpire in our lives. That's why it's important to be vigilant. Gentlemen, in order to understand, evaluate and heal black women, black men as a collective must work on uplifting themselves in every aspect of their lives (mentally emotionally, physically, financially, spiritually). When black women start to see how much you value and take care of yourself, most of them will not only be attracted to you, but they'll also become more motivated to improve themselves, especially if they want to fit into your life. Gentlemen when it comes to understanding, evaluating, and healing black women, the first thing you must learn how to do is elevate your mind and your spirit. If any woman is coming into your life to make you unstable and unhappy, leave the relationship. A man must be focused on higher things in life. In other words, it is our responsibility as men to make sure we are stable minded individuals. In addition to that, it is our responsibility to not intentionally bring instability or negativity into the woman's life. Keep in mind that women (particularly black women) go through a lot of mental, physical, financial, emotional, and spiritual hardships in life that causes them to be unstable. It's essential for men to provide guidance, stability, love and healing so that way the women can be more balanced. Thereafter maybe she can become a great consort.